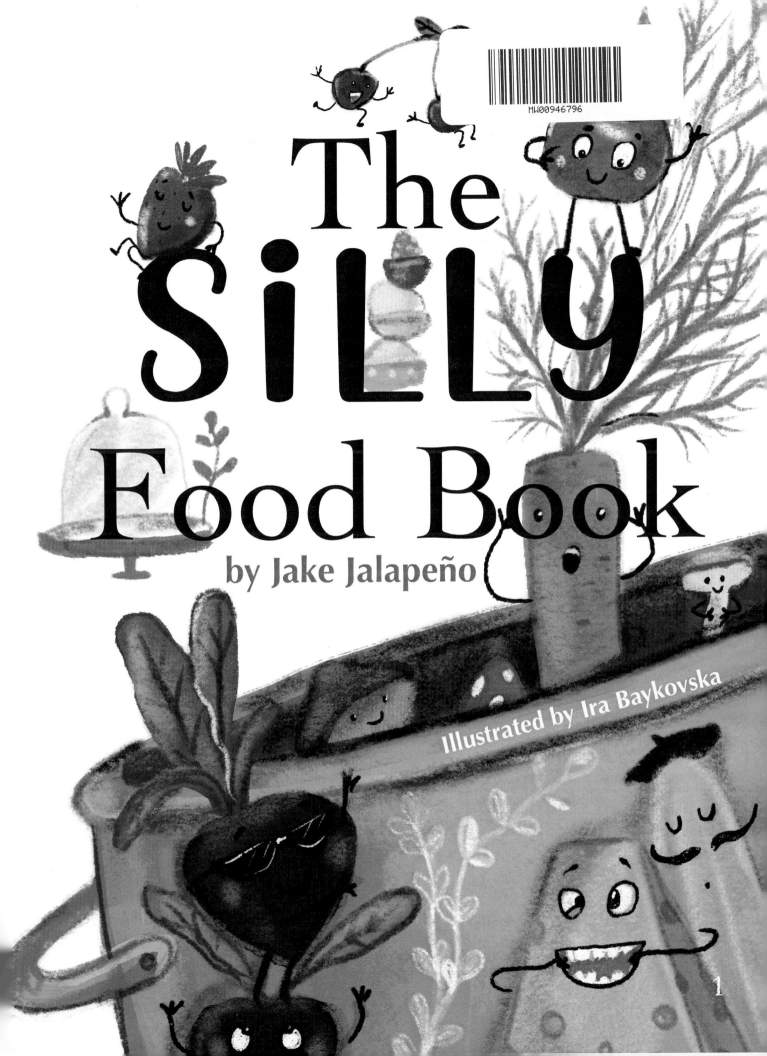

The SiLLy Food Book

by Jake Jalapeño

Illustrated by Ira Baykovska

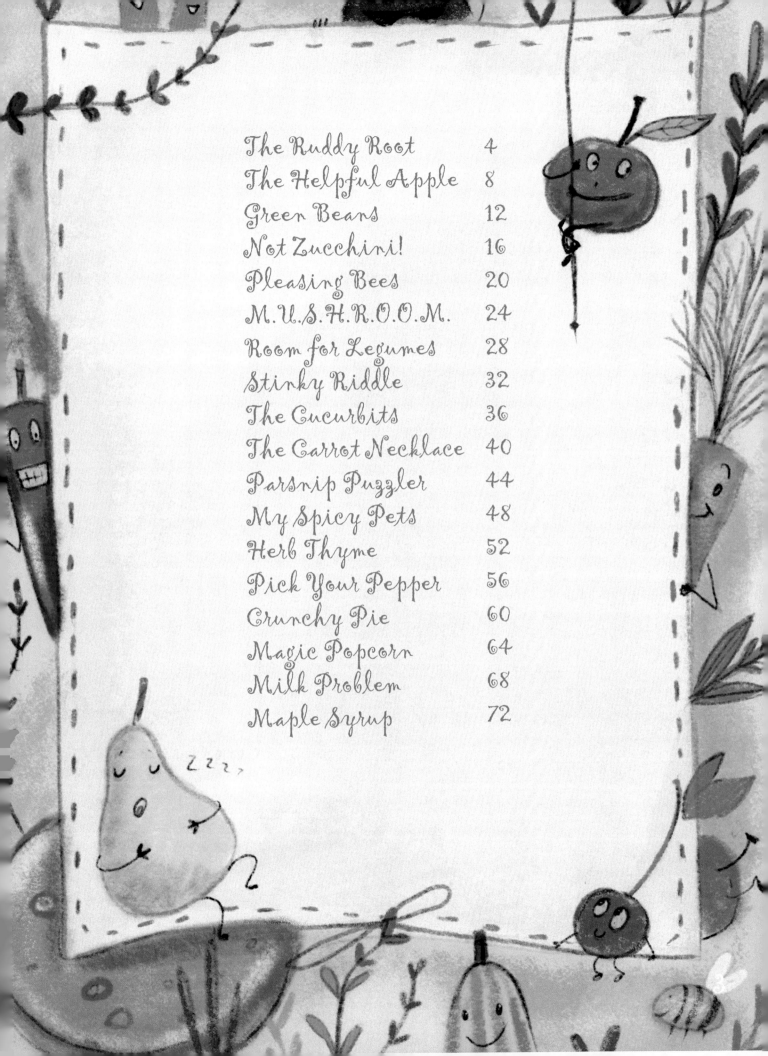

The Ruddy Root

The beet! The beet! Don't lose the beet!
The ruddy root
just can't be beat.

The beet! The beet! The sweetie beet.
The taproot queen
it's nice to meet.

4

The beet! The beet! A summer treat.
It grows in spring
and winter keeps.

The beet! The beet! With vibrant greens
so tall and lean
that you can eat.

The beet! The beet! It's good for me.
It's pickled and
a roasted treat.

The beet! The beet! Don't lose the beet!

What is a taproot? It is the long central root of a plant that grows deepest in the soil. Side roots branch off from this main root. Examples of taproots that we eat are carrots, beets, parsnips, turnips, and radishes.

Beets grow in many colors such as red, pink, orange, yellow, white, and even a red-and-white striped variety. No matter the color, the entire plant is edible, including roots, stems, and leaves.

Hot Buttered Beets

Time: 1 hour and 15 minutes, mostly unattended

Servings: 4

Skill Level: Easy

Ingredients

- 10-12 golf ball-sized beets
- 2 Tablespoons butter
- salt to taste
- ¼ cup chopped fresh herbs such as parsley, basil, or dill (optional)

Directions

1. If the beets have leaves, wash and trim the greens leaving an inch of stem on the beet.
2. Place beets in a medium saucepan and cover them with water, then bring to a boil. Boil beets for about 45 minutes or until tender when pierced with a fork.
3. Drain the beets and let cool for 5 minutes. Peel the beets under cool running water (the skins should slip off easily when rubbed with your hands).
4. Slice off the root and stem ends of the beet and discard. Slice the beets and return them to the saucepan with the butter over medium heat. Warm the beets for 5 minutes and stir them to coat with butter, adding a dash of salt. Remove the saucepan from the heat and add the chopped herbs. Serve.

The Helpful Apple

A chef was in the kitchen, thinking what to make,
when it occurred to him to try to make a cake.
Behind a wooden bowl, upon the counter's back,
a cheery and bright voice announced "I can do that!"

An apple's voice it was that the chef had heard,
but chatting with a fruit, he found to be absurd.
"Apples do not talk," the chef had slowly said.
"Perhaps I need a rest. I'll go lie down in bed."

"Oh, no, please don't!" the kindly eager fruit replied.
"For if you don't like cake, make me into a pie."
The chef stared blankly and did feel at such a loss.
Just then the apple ventured, "Maybe, just a sauce?"

"Make me into what you want to sink your tooth in,
including German cake that is called a Kuchen."
The startled chef replied "I don't know where to start.
You could be used for crumble, crisp, a bread or tart."

"I can do that!" the bright and useful apple cheered.
It was at this time that things started to get weird.
The chef, excited, cried out "I know what to do!
I'll be right back to show you my big plans for you!"

The apple patiently did ponder on the matter.
The chef returned with a pig upon a platter.
The porker's mouth was wide. The chef said "In you go."
A shocked and blushing apple said "I don't think so!"

What is a kuchen? Kuchen is the German word for cake, pronounced "koo-ken". Traditionally on Sundays, Germans gather with friends and family in the afternoon to enjoy kuchen with tea or coffee.

Many years ago, whole pigs were roasted, much like chickens are now. After the pig had been cooked, an apple would be put in its mouth as a sort of decoration.

Varieties of fruits or vegetables are sometimes called "heirloom". Heirloom simply means they have been around a long time, or they are old (but do not call your grandparents "heirlooms"!). Some names of heirloom apples are: Sheep's Nose, Cox's Orange Pippin, Gravenstein, Hudson's Golden Gem, Maiden's Blush, Northern Spy, Pitmaston Pineapple, Sops of Wine, and Winter Banana.

Baked Apples

Ingredients

4 apples (Jonathan, Braeburn, Honeycrisp, or other hard apple)

½ cup chopped almonds

4 Tablespoons raisins

1 ½ teaspoon cinnamon

2 Tablespoons butter

2 Tablespoons honey

Time: About 1 hour
Servings: 8
Skill Level: Easy

Directions

1. Preheat oven to 350° F. Cut apples in half and carefully cut or scoop out the core. Place apple halves into a 9×12 baking dish.
2. In a small bowl, combine almonds, raisins, cinnamon, and butter. Put a dollop or two of filling mixture on top of each apple half.
3. Bake apples, covered, for 20 minutes. Uncover and continue cooking 20 minutes longer or until the apples are soft.
4. Serve apple halves individually on a plate and drizzle with honey and sauce from the baking pan. (You may also add a scoop of ice cream if you ask your parents nicely!)

Green Beans

What if green beans were blue?
What do you think they'd do?

Could they grow to the sky
and match the blue up high?

Should white be how they grow,
they would get lost in snow.

I can't imagine gray
good-tasting any way.

Were crimson they instead,
they might be called "well-read".

I think that what I mean:
I'm glad green beans are green.

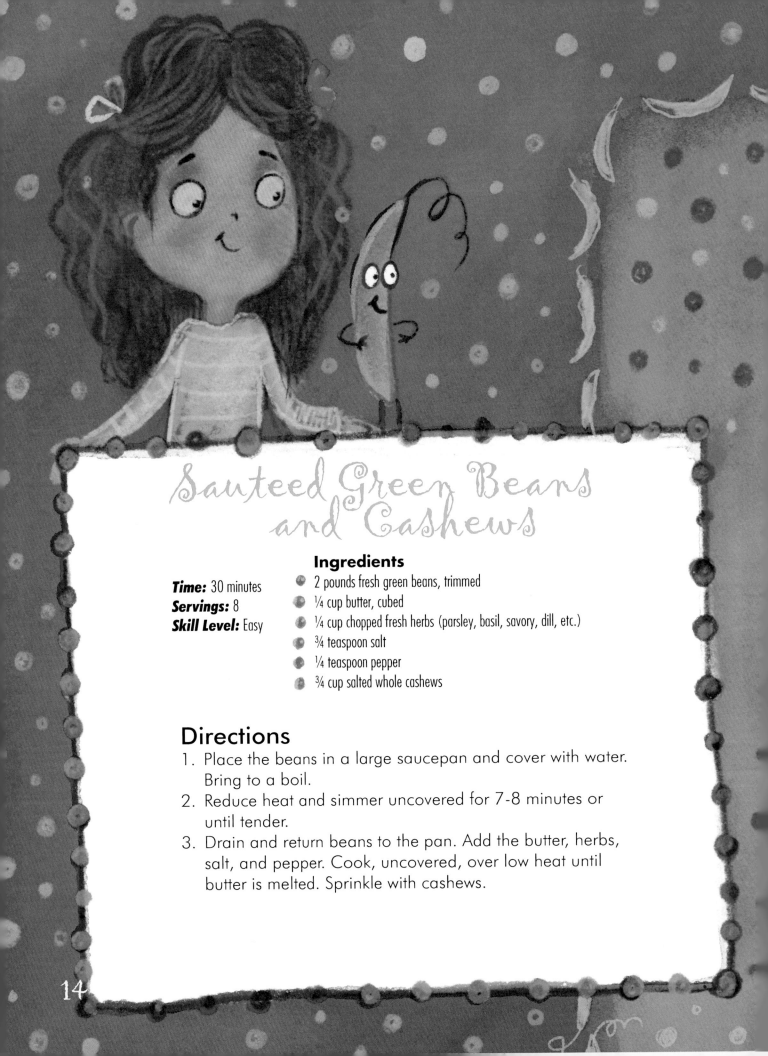

Sauteed Green Beans and Cashews

Time: 30 minutes
Servings: 8
Skill Level: Easy

Ingredients
- 2 pounds fresh green beans, trimmed
- ¼ cup butter, cubed
- ¼ cup chopped fresh herbs (parsley, basil, savory, dill, etc.)
- ¾ teaspoon salt
- ¼ teaspoon pepper
- ¾ cup salted whole cashews

Directions
1. Place the beans in a large saucepan and cover with water. Bring to a boil.
2. Reduce heat and simmer uncovered for 7-8 minutes or until tender.
3. Drain and return beans to the pan. Add the butter, herbs, salt, and pepper. Cook, uncovered, over low heat until butter is melted. Sprinkle with cashews.

Although Wisconsin is known for its cheese, it also grows more green beans than any other state in the nation.

January 6th is National Bean Day.

Fresh beans are also known as snap beans, wax beans, string beans, or pole beans. All of these types of beans can be used in the same way you would use green beans.

snap beans

wax beans

string beans

pole beans

Not Zucchini!

I heard a groan when it was fried.
Complaint was in the air.
The sour-faced children acted like
I had cooked up underwear.

"It's good for you, and it does have
plenty of manganese.
And if that's not enough, there are
vitamins B and C."

Loud groans and moans, and trying whines
surrounded me at once.
You'd think that I had asked them
to eat car parts for their lunch.

"I'll roast or fry or blend it fine,
if that is what it takes.
And I could even shred them up
to make some great pancakes."

And then one child dropped to the ground,
his senses out of reach.
He flapped his little fists just like
a whale that had been beached.

"Now listen up," I said. "There's no
more room for snotty moods.
You need to eat zucchini now
or no dessert for you!"

Now all is quiet, and I hear
chewing without a cry.
Perhaps the children should be told
dessert is eggplant pie.

Parmesan Zucchini

Time: 15 minutes
Servings: 4
Skill Level: Easy

Ingredients

2 medium zucchini or summer squash
1 teaspoon garlic powder
2 teaspoons dried herbs
(parsley, basil, oregano, etc.)
1 teaspoon salt
½ teaspoon pepper (optional)
2 Tablespoons olive oil
1 cup parmesan cheese

Directions

1. Preheat oven to 450° F.
2. Slice zucchini into 1/4 inch discs and place into a bowl. Add garlic powder, herbs, salt, pepper, and olive oil. Mix until the zucchini slices are well-coated.
3. Place slices on a cookie sheet and top each one with a little parmesan cheese. Bake for 15 minutes. For the last 2 minutes, turn on the broiler until the cheese is bubbly and slightly brown. Serve.

Zucchini is called "courgette" (koor-zhet) in France, and "baby marrow" in South Africa.

Zucchini is a type of summer squash. Other summer squashes include pattypan, crookneck, zephyr, round, and cousa. Zucchini and summer squash can be used interchangeably in recipes.

Do you think you could tell the difference between zucchini pie and apple pie? Recipes for "mock apple pie" or "zucchini apple pie" use zucchini instead of the apples. The results can be so convincing that people think they are eating apple pie. (As a child, the author of this book was fooled!)

Over 90 percent of a zucchini is water.

Pleasing Bees
(Limericks)

Bees are awesome creatures you know!
With nectar that makes honey flow,
they will take no chance,
do a waggle dance,
so other bees know where to go.

Their wings seem so small at first sight
and crashing down looks like their plight.
With shortened wing-strokes,
these magical folks
take plump little bodies to flight.

These bees are attracted to flowers
but they do not fly in rain showers.
In their hive they stay
and patiently wait,
then bring back their pollen for hours.

With thousands of bees in a hive
one wonders that they can survive.
It is a sad song
they won't live too long;
their days are about forty-five.

These creatures work hard every day;
they don't even take time to play.
They store up the nectar,
these expert collectors-
they are sweet flying friends, I say!

When bees find flowers and return to the hive, they will do a wiggly dance over and over while other bees crowd around to watch. This dance will tell the other bees where to fly to locate the flowers.

An average bee flaps its wings over 180 times per second.

Perfectly edible honey that is over 3000 years old has been found in Egyptian tombs.

Honey Roasted Almonds

Time: 30 minutes
Servings: Depends on how many
you want to eat!
Skill Level: Easy

Ingredients

- 1 Tablespoon butter
- 2 Tablespoons honey
- 2 cups raw unsalted almonds
- ½ teaspoon sea salt

Directions

1. Preheat oven to 300° F.
2. Place the butter and honey in a glass baking dish. Heat in the oven until melted, about 2 minutes.
3. Add the nuts, mix, and roast, stirring every 10 minutes, for about 30 minutes total.
4. Remove the nuts from the pan and spread them evenly on wax paper or parchment paper. Sprinkle with the salt. Allow to cool and crisp up, about 20 minutes. Eat them up…and maybe share with someone.

M.U.S.H.R.O.O.M.

Mushrooms come in many forms.
Usually they're in the store.
Sometimes you can find them dried.
Have them roasted, stewed, or fried.
Refrain from eating in the wild
Or you could be sick a while.
Oyster, Shiitake, and Crimini,
Morel, Button, and Porcini.

Crispy Roasted Mushrooms

Time: 1 hour
Servings: 8
Skill Level: Easy

Ingredients

- 1 pound roughly chopped mixed mushrooms (oyster, button, cremini, shiitake, portobello, etc.)
- ¼ cup extra virgin olive oil
- 3 cloves garlic, minced
- salt and black pepper to taste
- ⅛ cup fresh parsley, chopped

Directions

1. Preheat oven to 450° F.
2. In a large bowl, toss the mushrooms along with the olive oil, garlic, salt, and pepper.
3. Spread the mushrooms out on a baking sheet lined with foil. Roast for about 30-40 minutes until the mushrooms are brown and crispy. Stir them at least once during the roasting time. Garnish with fresh parsley.

One particular variety of mushroom called "chicken of the woods" is supposed to taste like fried chicken. It is easily recognizable by its large size and impressive vibrant orange and yellow colors.
It grows in "shelves" on the sides of hardwood trees like oak, cherry, or beech.

Truffles, which are a fungus, grow underneath the soil at the base of trees. They are rare and can only be found at certain times of the year. They have a strong aroma. Many people use dogs or pigs to locate them by sniffing. White truffles can cost over $4000 per pound.

Yartsa gunbu is a fungus found in parts of China and Tibet. This fungus grows from a dead caterpillar and can be more expensive to buy than gold.

Room for Legumes

Stack my dish
sky-high, I wish,
with legumes.

Ham and peas.
Oh, yes! Please!
I'm in the mood.

Chickpeas make
falafel great,
and hummus too.

Refried beans
with lots of cheese,
I treasure you.

Chili may,
on a cold day,
warm you all through.

Bean soup hot,
served from a pot,
is comfort food.

Sweet beans baked
can really make
me almost swoon.

Peanuts seem
to be a dream
that has come true.

Beans and rice.
Now that is nice.
Do I have room?

What's that sound
I heard just now?
Did I just toot?

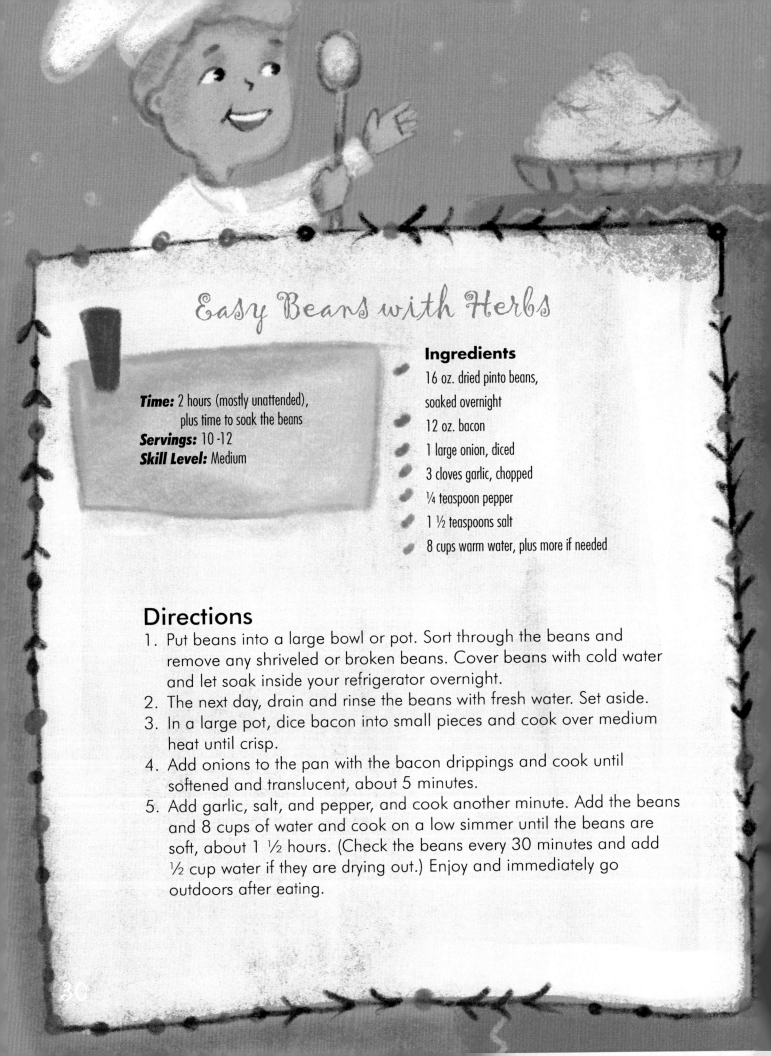

Easy Beans with Herbs

Time: 2 hours (mostly unattended),
plus time to soak the beans
Servings: 10-12
Skill Level: Medium

Ingredients

- 16 oz. dried pinto beans, soaked overnight
- 12 oz. bacon
- 1 large onion, diced
- 3 cloves garlic, chopped
- ¼ teaspoon pepper
- 1 ½ teaspoons salt
- 8 cups warm water, plus more if needed

Directions

1. Put beans into a large bowl or pot. Sort through the beans and remove any shriveled or broken beans. Cover beans with cold water and let soak inside your refrigerator overnight.
2. The next day, drain and rinse the beans with fresh water. Set aside.
3. In a large pot, dice bacon into small pieces and cook over medium heat until crisp.
4. Add onions to the pan with the bacon drippings and cook until softened and translucent, about 5 minutes.
5. Add garlic, salt, and pepper, and cook another minute. Add the beans and 8 cups of water and cook on a low simmer until the beans are soft, about 1 ½ hours. (Check the beans every 30 minutes and add ½ cup water if they are drying out.) Enjoy and immediately go outdoors after eating.

"Legume" is a general term used to describe the seeds of plants from the legume plant family, which includes beans, peas, lentils, and peanuts.

Do beans really make you toot? Yes, they do! When we eat beans, our bodies try to digest them. A sugar in the beans does not digest easily. When this sugar meets bacteria in our intestines, they form a gas. "Tooting" is this gas coming out of our body.

Beans come in all sorts of shapes, sizes, and colors. They have many unusual and interesting names such as Soldier, Cherokee Trail of Tears, Jacob's Cattle, Lazy Wife, Tiger Eye, Bird Egg Blue, and Yin Yang.

Stinky Riddle

They come in wheels, but they don't roll.
People like when they get old.

Although they're sharp and they can't cut,
you get a slice when it's split up.

The milk comes from cow, sheep and goat,
yak, reindeer, camel, buffalo.

They are not dirty but at times
people need to wash their rinds.

The answer to this mystery?
Take a picture and say "_____".

Have you ever wondered why some cheese is orange but others are white? Cows naturally produce white or slightly yellow milk, especially if they are grazing on green grass. However, to give cheese an intense orange color most cheesemakers use annatto, which is a food coloring produced from the seeds of the achiote tree.

Radish Cheese Sandwich

Time: 10 minutes
Servings: 1
Skill Level: Super Easy

Ingredients

- 2-3 radishes, sliced
- 2 slices of bread
- butter (room temperature)
- 1 slice of your favorite cheese
- salt to taste
- mayonnaise (optional)

Directions

1. Butter two slices of bread. Spread mayonnaise on one slice, if you are using it.
2. Cover the other slice of bread with radishes. Sprinkle salt on the radishes. Add cheese. Put the halves together.

Scrambled Cheese

1. hdacedr
2. nespmara
3. zellzormaa
4. bier
5. made
6. feat
7. blocy
8. wisss
9. oudag

Answers

1. cheddar 2. parmesan 3. mozzarella 4. brie 5. edam 6. feta
7. colby 8. swiss 9. gouda

The Cucurbits
(a cucumber's family)

The Cucurbit clan
is complex and very large.
And many times it's tricky
telling who's in charge.

Cucumber has an uncle.
Pumpkin is his name.
Cousin Cantaloupe is
a sweet and charming dame.

Now his Great Grandpa Gourd-
whom you may have met-
talks of Aunt Zucchini,
also called Courgette.

There was a niece named, Loofah,
though I am not certain.
You can know for sure if
you ask Grandma Gherkin

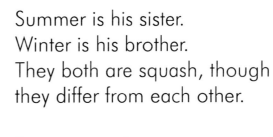

Summer is his sister.
Winter is his brother.
They both are squash, though
they differ from each other.

Some are soft, some are rough.
Sweet they are sometimes.
And their whole family tree
is actually a vine.

Cucumbers are effective at soothing sunburnt skin. You can mash or blend cucumbers into a paste and apply it to your skin, or you can even put thin slices on those hurting burnt spots.

Have you ever wondered why people use the phrase "cool as a cucumber"? Since cucumbers are up to 95% water, they stay cooler on the inside than they do on the outside.

Muskmelon, cucumbers, gourds, pumpkins, zucchini, winter squash, as well as other fruits, belong to the Cucurbit (kyoo-kur-bit) family. They are all different from each other in appearance, just like you and your family all have different appearances and names, but are still related.

Cucumber Salad

Time: 15 minutes
Servings: 4-6
Skill Level: Super Easy

Ingredients

- 1 pint cherry tomatoes, halved
- 1 large cucumber, peeled and diced
- 8 oz. mozzarella balls
- 10-12 fresh basil leaves, chopped fine
- 2 Tablespoons olive oil
  (extra virgin, cold-pressed is best)
- 1 Tablespoon balsamic vinegar
- 1 garlic clove, minced
- salt and pepper, to taste

Directions

1. In a large bowl, combine tomatoes, cucumber, mozzarella, and basil leaves.
2. In a separate small bowl, whisk together the olive oil, vinegar, garlic, salt, and pepper. Pour it over the tomato-mozzarella mixture and mix well. Eat up!

The Carrot Necklace

Mary had a carrot necklace and she wore it with such pride.
Made of juicy bright orange carrots, it did catch me by surprise.

On her graceful neck two dozen roots were fastened with a cord;
edible adornments of this sort just could not be ignored.

I went up to her and said "I certainly don't mean to pry.
What's the reason for your necklace? Take the time to tell me why."

"Prized and dear they are to me," with smile she eagerly declared it.
"These two dozen roots are my beloved 24 carrots!"

Gold is graded by the measurement called "karats". The most expensive and purest form of gold is 24 karats.

The famous wildflower called Queen Anne's Lace is also known as "wild carrot". Many times you can find one little purple flower in the center of the many clusters of white ones. However, stick to eating the carrots you find in the store since wild carrots can be confused with other poisonous plants.

Holtville, California hosts a carrot festival every year that includes cooking contests, races, artwork, a tractor show, parade, and a carnival.

Carrot Salad

Time: 15 minutes
Servings: 8 servings
Skill Level: Easy

Ingredients

5-6 large carrots
½ cup raisins (optional)
1 large apple, peeled and chopped
1 cup roughly chopped walnuts (optional)
½ cup mayonnaise

Directions
1. Peel and grate the carrots.
2. Put all the ingredients into a bowl and mix well. That's it!

Parsnip Puzzler

I'm in the mood
for some good food,
but there's only parsnips in my fridge.
Maybe I'll make
a parsnip shake?
That seems not right, not even a tidge.
Parsnip doughnuts
I would try, but
only if I was in a tight pinch.

It is a test,
I think at best,
to have parsnip jelly on my toast.
It's not much fun,
no one would come
if invited to a parsnip roast.
And, I must say,
parsnip pate`
Would never be cause for me to boast.

Now what to do?
Can I ask you?
I have not a thought on what to make.
I'll try again.
But in the end,
I don't know what it's going to take.
Wait just a bit…
I've thought of it.
Parsnips and BACON, for goodness sake!

Parsnips used to be popular around the world. They were roasted, mashed, pureed, fried, and used in soups, jams, wine, and medicine.
Pigs and cows were also fed parsnips to keep them healthy and strong (why?). In the mid-1800s, parsnips decreased in popularity as potatoes became widely grown.

Parsnips were often used as a sweetener in foods before sugar became common.

 Roasted Parsnips

Time: 1 hour, 15 minutes
Servings: 6
Skill Level: Medium

Ingredients

2 pounds parsnips

8 oz. bacon (save the drippings!)

½ teaspoon salt

½ teaspoon pepper

Directions

1. Heat the oven to 425 degrees.
2. Cut bacon into 1-inch pieces, fry in a pan over low heat for 15-20 minutes, stirring frequently.
3. While the bacon is cooking, peel the parsnips and trim off both ends. Cut them into roughly 1-2 inch chunks.
4. When the bacon is brown and crisp, turn off the heat and remove the bacon pieces to a bowl with a slotted spoon.
5. Pour the bacon drippings into a 9x13 roasting pan (be careful, the drippings are hot!), toss in the parsnips, sprinkle with salt and pepper and stir until all the pieces are coated with fat. Spread the pieces evenly in the roasting pan.
6. Roast for 35-45 minutes, stirring every 15 minutes, until the pieces are browned. Remove the pan from the oven and stir in the bacon pieces.

My Spicy Pets

My dog, **Coriander**, for **ginger** has a taste.
And **Nutmeg**, my orange cat, will lick up **cardamom**.
My parrot, **Juniper**, turns up his nose to **mace**.
He's happy chewing on a stick of **cinnamon**.

My trusty steed called **Pepper** rolls in **turmeric**.
The hamster, **Cumin**, nibbles nightly on **saffron**.
My cow, named **Clove**, for a fancy pasture picnic,
will gladly ruminate on **garlic** by the ton.

48

The lovely backyard goat, whom we call **Caraway**,
will eat most anything, but really loves **allspice**.
Piggy **Paprika** is most happy all the day
with **fennel** in his water; it has to be on ice.

But my kids no matter what is on the table,
cover all their food with **ketchup** if they're able.

49

Spiced Butter

Time: 5 minutes, plus time to chill
Servings: How much do you like butter?
Skill Level: Super Easy

Ingredients

1 stick (4 oz.) unsalted butter, room temperature

1 teaspoon cinnamon

1 tablespoon maple syrup

Directions

1. Put all ingredients together in a bowl and blend with a hand-held beater until smooth.
2. Transfer the butter onto wax paper and roll into a log shape. Let the log of butter sit in the fridge for 2 hours.
3. Slice and serve on toast, sweet potatoes, waffles, cornbread, pancakes, winter squash, oatmeal, rice pudding, or anything you like.

The most expensive spice in the world is saffron, valued at over $5000 dollars per pound. Saffron is the stigma of a crocus flower. It takes 50,000 to 75,000 crocus flowers to produce one pound of dried saffron.

Cinnamon, grown in warm climates near the Equator, is the dried and ground inner bark of a tree that belongs to the Laurel family. Sri Lanka produces much of the world's cinnamon.

Black pepper, one of the most commonly used spices in the world, grows as small clusters of green berries harvested from a leafy vine. The berries are dried in the sun and turn a black color. They are not from the same plant as colored bell peppers.

51

Basil

Sage

Thyme

Lemon balm

Bay leaves

Savory

Chives

Herb Thyme

My day's well with **basil**.
My food thrives with lots of **chives**.
I'm sentimental about my **fennel**.
I won't part with **parsley**.
No **dill** makes me ill.
I'm in a rage without **sage**.
It's so scary with no **rosemary**.
I can't go a stint minus **mint**.
Without **savory**, it's sheer bravery.
I'm a wreck, you know, without **oregano**.
And I may grieve with no **bay leaves**.
Minus **cilantro**, I just will not go.
No **lemon balm**? I won't be calm.
If I'm mad, thereupon, I need **tarragon**.
It makes me saddish, sans **horseradish**.
I'm out of **thyme**. No more rhyme.

What is the difference between
an herb and a spice?
An herb is the green, leafy part of the
plant. A spice can come from the root,
stem, seed, fruit, flower, or bark of
a plant.

Spice

Herb

Mint Tea

Time: 15 minutes
Servings: 1
Skill Level: Super Easy

Ingredients

water

12 fresh mint leaves

½ teaspoon honey

Directions

1. Bring water to a boil. If you have a tea ball or strainer, put the mint inside of it and put the strainer in your cup.
2. Once the water has boiled, take it off the stove and let it rest 5 minutes. Pour the water into your cup and let the tea steep for 10 minutes.
3. Remove the tea strainer. Mix in 1/2 teaspoon of honey.

Mint is a common herb used to flavor tea, ice cream, chocolate, vegetables, sauces, meats, fruit, toothpaste, soap, household cleaners, medicine, and even bug repellents.

Pick Your Pepper

I like them hot.
Would you say not?
You might say "No
jalapeño!"

You like them sweet
without the heat.
No need to earn
a scalding burn.

Capsaicin sting
is not your thing.
I like to feign
there is no pain.

Though it's astute
to call them "fruit",
I don't insert
them in dessert.

A fruit is the part of the plant that has the seeds in it. A vegetable is any other part of the plant we eat that does not have the seeds – the stem, leaves, roots, flowers. Peppers, tomatoes, pumpkins, cucumbers, and many other "vegetables" are correctly called… fruits.

Capsaicin (cap-say-sin) is the chemical found in hot peppers that makes them HOT.

Peppers come in an astonishing array of colors including green, yellow, red, orange, purple, white, brown, and even striped. All green peppers will eventually turn another color if left on the plant long enough.

Pepper Poppers

Time: 40 minutes
Servings: 8-10
Skill Level: Medium (A little parent help needed)

Ingredients

1 pound of pork sausage

12-15 small "snack-size" or "mini" peppers
(jalapeños work too…if you are brave!)

8 oz. cream cheese

1 cup parmesan cheese, shredded

3 cloves garlic, crushed

salt to taste

Directions

1. Preheat the oven to 375° F.
2. Brown the pork sausage in a skillet over medium heat. Drain the fat and let the meat cool.
3. Meanwhile, cut the peppers in half lengthwise, scoop out the seeds and remove the stems.
4. Combine sausage, cream cheese, parmesan, garlic, and salt in a bowl and mix well. Fill each pepper half with the mixture and place them in a baking pan.
5. Bake for 20-25 minutes, until the peppers are soft and the filling is starting to brown slightly.

Crunchy Pie

I had made a cherry pie
but didn't take out the pits.
Now we all eat up dessert
and everyone just spits.

Cherry (not crunchy) Pie

Time: 30 minutes, plus time for cooling
Servings: 8
Skill Level: Medium (might need a little help)

Ingredients

Crust

2 cups pecan pieces

4 tablespoons salted butter, melted

12 dates, finely chopped

Filling

4 cups whole pitted fresh sweet cherries or 1 ½ lbs thawed frozen sweet cherries (with juice)

¼ cup honey, plus 2 tsp for the whipped cream

1 tablespoon freshly squeezed lemon juice

¼ cup cornstarch

¼ cup cold water

½ teaspoon almond extract

8 oz. heavy whipping cream

Directions

1. Preheat the oven to 350 F.
2. Place pecan pieces into a food processor. Pulse until the nuts are a rough paste. Add the melted butter and dates and blend until mixed evenly.
3. Transfer the mixture to a 9-inch pie pan and press the mixture with your fingers or back of a spoon to cover the bottom and sides of the pan.
4. Place in the oven and bake for 10-12 minutes, checking to make sure the crust does not brown too much.

For the filling

1. Place cherries into a large saucepan. Add 1/4 cup honey, lemon juice, cornstarch, water, and almond extract, then stir to coat. Turn on the heat to medium. Cook the filling, stirring often, until glossy and thickened, about 5 - 10 minutes. Remove the pan from the heat and let the filling cool completely.
2. Place the cream and 2 teaspoons of honey in a bowl and beat with an electric mixer or a whisk until cream holds stiff peaks.
3. Once the cherry filling has cooled, pour it into the crust and spread evenly. Spread the whipped cream over the cherries. Share the pie.

Egyptians, Romans, and eventually Europeans all had versions of pie. The crust was not always eaten, but served as a dish in which to bake the filling. This dish was called a "coffin" or "coffyn".

Pizza is sometimes referred to as pie. Pizza is America's favorite food and pepperoni is the most popular topping.

Apple is considered America's favorite pie; pumpkin is second.

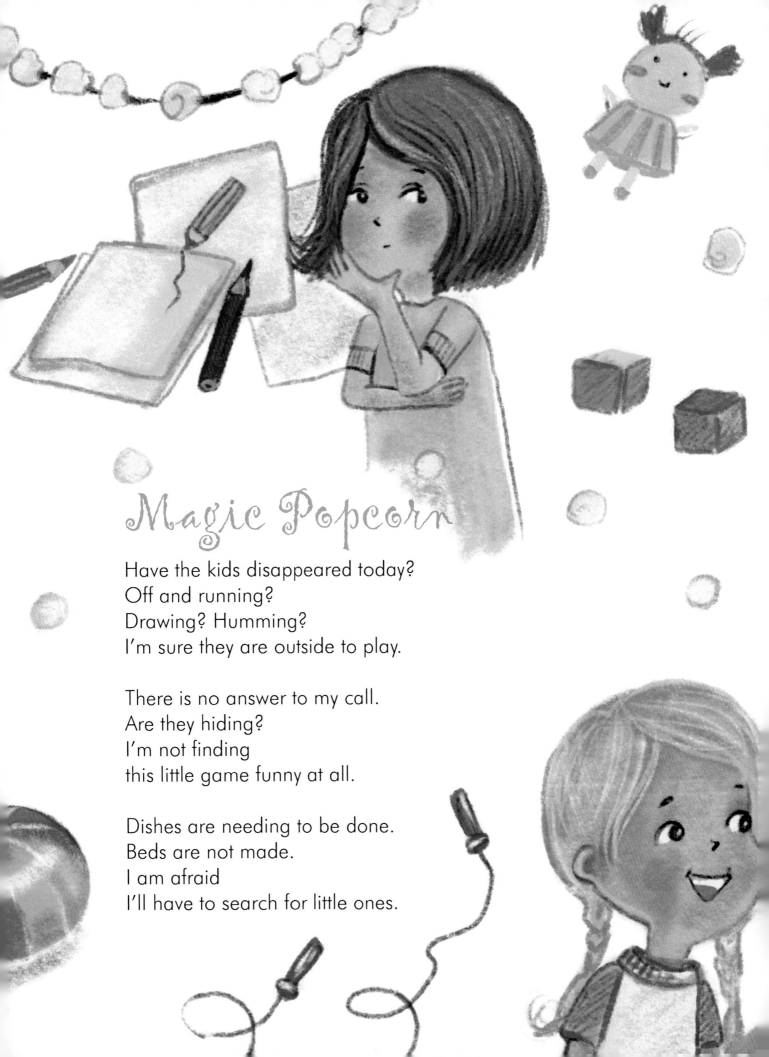

Magic Popcorn

Have the kids disappeared today?
Off and running?
Drawing? Humming?
I'm sure they are outside to play.

There is no answer to my call.
Are they hiding?
I'm not finding
this little game funny at all.

Dishes are needing to be done.
Beds are not made.
I am afraid
I'll have to search for little ones.

But wait, I think I need not search -
a sound, I reckon,
that will beckon
children from corners of the earth.

They race to the kitchen, stopping.
They plead with eyes
for the hot prize.
Yes, they heard the popcorn popping!

The little town of Sac City, Iowa is known for the world's largest popcorn ball, standing over eight feet tall and weighing in at 9370 pounds!

Popcorn became increasingly popular during the Great Depression. Popcorn was a very inexpensive food, selling for 5 or 10 cents a bag. It was one of the few foods even poor people could eat.

Each popcorn kernel contains a small amount of water. When heated this water turns to steam and causes an explosion, which makes…popcorn!

Magic Popcorn

Time: 15 minutes
Servings: 4
Skill Level: Easy

Ingredients
- ½ cup popcorn kernels
- 2 tablespoons butter
- 2 tablespoons coconut oil
- 1 tablespoon honey
- salt to taste

Directions
1. Pop the popcorn on the stovetop or use an air popper. Put popcorn in a large bowl.
2. Melt the butter, coconut oil and honey in a small pot on the stove over low heat, mixing as it melts.
3. Slowly pour half the butter oil mixture over the popcorn in a fine drizzle. Salt the popcorn and mix it with a spoon.
4. Pour the rest of the butter oil mixture over the popcorn and taste to see if you need more salt. Run to your room and eat it all! Oh…bring a napkin!

Milk Problem

The mother milk said to the father milk one night,
"Our son is troubled. I'm concerned. Is he alright?"

"What do you mean? What is the cause for your concern?
He's faithful, honest, true. Your trust he's worked to earn."

"He's not as sweet, he sits around. He smells a tad.
He won't be friends with cookies, saying they are bad.

He hangs around with cheese, is courting sour cream.
I heard he bought a book to try to learn some Greek.

Does he need this culture that isn't on the farm?
His friends are probiotics! Why aren't you alarmed?"

"Our boy is different now and has no aim to hurt.
We should be very proud he's changing to yogurt."

Making yogurt from milk requires fermentation. Good bacteria added to the milk causes the milk to ferment.
This process keeps the milk from spoiling. The milk changes in flavor and texture and the result is yogurt.

Other fermented foods are cheese, sauerkraut, kefir, kimchi, kombucha, sourdough bread, beer, and wine.

Yogurt Sundaes

Time: 10 minutes
Servings: As many as needed
Skill Level: Super Easy

Ingredients

- plain yogurt (preferably full fat)
- maple syrup or honey (optional)
- fresh fruit (bananas, peaches, berries, apples, etc.)
- dried fruit (raisins, cranberries, apricots, figs, dates, etc.)
- dried coconut
- nuts (almonds, cashews, pecans, walnuts, etc.)
- cinnamon
- granola
- chocolate chips (maybe just a few)
- seeds (sunflower, pumpkin, sesame, etc.)

Directions

Put about ½ cup of yogurt in a bowl. Sprinkle on your favorite toppings. Done.

71

Maple Syrup

(Inspired by "The Raven" by Edgar Allan Poe)

One day upon a winter clear, the leafless woods so austere,
the sun had pierced the pale gray sky making morning out of night.
The towering trees stood so proud, in ribboned snow below the clouds,
when a man came to tapping, tapping maple trees in sight.
With his spiles he was tapping maple trees while there was light.
He went tapping until night.

Their veins pierced and clear sap streaming, into metal buckets gleaming,
the trees stood still, unmoving, soldiers at attention statue-like.
Days went by, the buckets filling, winter nights had grown less chilling.
Spring did cast out winter slowly, sympathetic to the robin's plight.
Winter now had lost most surely it's bold and furious frozen bite.
Spring was here. Oh, what a sight!

The smoky smell of wood burning, the boiling steam of sap churning
drifted on endless breezes to heavenly unseen heights.
The sap once clear grew golden thick, to every surface began to stick.
Once again the evening flowed, and cool air settled on the night,
manifesting frozen breath by fading embers of firelight.
Morning would return so bright.

The kitchen table awaited graces, plates were set out to their spaces.
People round the table - hungry, bright eyed, sleepy - were packed in tight.
Pancakes, golden, piled up high, were soon adorned with sweet supply
of nectar from the maple trees, that made breakfast a pure delight.
The young ones watched as it was poured, and with enormous appetite,
quoth the children "Oh, alright!"

It takes around 40 gallons of sap to make 1 gallon of maple syrup. Sap flow occurs in the springtime in cool climates when the nights are below freezing and the daytime temperatures get above freezing. People will generally drill a shallow hole in the side of a tree and put a small tube in the hole, and then sap will flow out from the tube into a bucket or bag. This tube is called a "spile".

74

Maple Syrup Cornbread

Time: 40 minutes
Servings: 8
Skill Level: Easy

Ingredients

1 cup all-purpose flour

1 cup yellow cornmeal

1 Tablespoon baking powder

1 teaspoon salt

1 cup milk

¼ cup butter, melted

2 eggs

⅓ cup of maple syrup (used after cornbread is baked)

Directions

1. Preheat the oven to 425° F.
2. Lightly grease an 8"x8" square, or 9" round baking pan.
3. In a medium-sized mixing bowl, mix together the flour, cornmeal, baking powder, and salt until well combined.
4. In a small bowl, whisk together the milk, melted butter, and eggs. Add to the dry ingredients. Stir until just moistened.
5. Pour the batter into the prepared pan. Bake for 20-25 minutes, until lightly golden, and a toothpick inserted comes out clean.
6. Remove from the oven and pour the maple syrup over the cornbread in a steady slow stream. Serve warm.

About the Author

Jake Jalapeno loves to grow, cook, eat and talk about food, but not all at the same time. Jake has very fond memories of being in the garden and kitchen as a youngster.

Jake and his wife, Heather, owned and operated "The Garden of Weedin'", a small organic farm in Wisconsin for 8 years. Jake also served as an Urban Farm Manager and Culinary Coordinator for Nourish, a non-profit food education organization in Sheboygan Falls.

His hobbies include sports, strategy board games, enjoying the outdoors, and cooking.

Jake, Heather, and their five little "poppers" live in Wisconsin.

jakejalapeno1@gmail.com

About the Illustrator

Ira Baykovska is a children's book illustrator and a big fan of food. She loves to cook and thanks to "The Silly Cook Book" rhymes, the process of preparing any dish will be a lot more fun and enjoyable from now on.

Ira has been drawing for as long as she can remember and sometimes cannot believe that this hobby has become her life-long career.

She has been working as a freelance illustrator since 2014 and has illustrated more than 20 books for kids.

Ira has a degree in Graphic Design and currently lives and works in Lviv, Ukraine.

Visit Ira's website **www.baykovska.com**

Made in United States
North Haven, CT
07 October 2023

42482937R00044